Woman On A Journey
30-day devotional

Tracy Youngston

Woman On A Journey
Copyright © 2021 Tracy Youngston

ISBN: 979-8-9854561-0-3

Table of contents

Table of contents

Hey Girl

Welcome aboard! Please take your seat and get comfortable. Better yet, don't get too comfortable; just put your seat belt on and try to enjoy the ride.

My name is Tracy Youngston, a child of Haitian Immigrant parents. I was a teen mom, a fatherless child, and a defiant little being. I've dealt with depression, insecurities, self-hate, dimming by light because it made people uncomfortable; I've had good days and bad days, and days that look like crap. That comparison syndrome is real, the imposter syndrome couldn't be my bigger downfall, and the lack of belief damn (yeah, I said it because that's how real it was for me). Damn, it nearly took me out completely. I've lived from hotel to hotel, even lived a year without my own children, I've been broke (in the negative), lost myself, loved a man more than I loved myself AND GOD, and almost lost my mind.

I say all that because we identify ourselves with what we've been through, who we were, and our circumstances. I'm pretty sure many can relate on more than one occasion with what I listed above; however, I am also here to remind you that you can rewrite your narrative by allowing God to be the pilot of your journey.

xoxo
t

I went through this process, screaming and hollering. I ask God, "Are you serious right now?" or cracking jokes like "Oh, so you think you're funny?" For everything that I said to myself or believed from the enemy, He literally took it and said, "This is what I said about you." Just imagine when your natural father reconfirms how beautiful you are and how much he believes in you. That will melt any daughter's heart into submission.

Intro

As women, our identity is something we are not truly taught how to find and/or appreciate. We are taught many things but somehow, that seemed to be left off the checklist.

Identity is the collective aspect of characteristics by which a thing or person is definitively recognized or known. Our parents, community, environment, and experiences all make up those collective pieces that meshed and made you, you. Our journey as women sometimes causes us to lose sight of who we are and whose we are. I'm just saying, we tend to take care of EVERYBODY ELSE and leave US behind.

But somebody loved you, me, us so much that He thought about us before we were conceived and even appointed us to the nations (Jeremiah. 1:5). He created us to be fearfully and wonderfully made (Psalms 139:14). One who knew the plans He had for us (Jeremiah. 29:11).

Journey with me (Stewardess) and God (The Pilot) as we travel through how He sees his collections as masterpieces and RECLAIM our identity.

Really be intentional about this! I've given you room to begin this journey by emptying your heart. Revealing those things that keep you bound, awake at night, those cry showers (I know those too well, especially if you have kids), screaming in the car asking God why. Yep, honey, those things. Find a quiet time to do this.

IT IS TIME YOU DO THIS FOR YOU!

_____

_____

_____

_____

_____

_____

_____

_____

_____

_____

_____

_____

What are those lies you believe about yourself?

It's okay, tears are a part of your beautification process,

_____

_____

_____

_____

_____

_____

_____

_____

_____

_____

_____

_____

Start declaring some new beliefs about who you are.

Day 1

Who Do I Think I Am?

For a season of my life, I battled with having a settled, firm acknowledgement of who I was AND who I was in Christ. As I sat down one day scratching my head, it hit me. I have been so engulfed in my roles and titles that grown Tracy didn't know who she was. (I don't know if I am the only one who suffered from the adult epiphany syndrome but better late than never).

So, my life went something like this: remembering my elementary school years, to being an abandoned child (middle school), to being a whole mother (high school), and to being married in (early twenties). Never was I taught to invest in who I was, who I am, and who I am called to be. I would look in the mirror and ask the reflection a question that went something like this:

"WHO ARE YOU?!"

This question would soon be followed by tears and more self-hated emotions and thoughts. I remember wanting to commit suicide because I was so desperate for an answer till that even became depressing.

xoxo
pg 1

Until one day...............hunty two snaps.......

My First Pastor Angel Thomas (Beacon of Light Empowerment Center) taught me "Mirror Ministry." Mirror Ministry is when you can face yourself in the mirror and look deep inside those broken eyes.

Uggghhhhh, have anyone ever tried this?!!! I went the first time but couldn't do it. The second time I cried so much, I was tired and needed a nap. The third, I asked God for His grace in revealing my hurt, my insecurities, and my pain. From that moment, I was able not only to face myself and all my nasty truth, but I was able to speak life back into my life.

My favorite scripture at that time was "I praise you, for I am fearfully and wonderfully made. [a] Wonderful are your works; my soul knows it very well." Psalm 139:14

You probably say this verse so dang fast till you don't even digest its true meaning, heck I didn't.

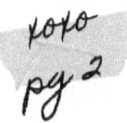

xoxo
pg 2

The biggest takeaway is the last piece of the verse, "my soul knows it very well." This means there's no second-guessing, questioning, or even allowing anyone else to say anything on the contrary. There's no hiccup in who you are, what you do, and what you can do; it's pure precision. Now I'm going to give you time to read it again.

Prayer: God, I'm here. In need of some fine-tuning and mirror ministry of who I am. I became a person that was clothed by my pain, hurt, guilt, shame, or by simply being a people pleaser. However, today, I say no more. Daddy, I don't want to continue to miss this opportunity to become this fearless and wonderful masterpiece of your creation. Help me to see what you see, whisper in my ears so I can hear your confirmations about who I am and allow those things to be everything that my soul knows very well. Let me not be moved by imposter syndrome, comparison syndrome, or whatever other self-diagnosis that is made outside of your will for my life. Allow me to embrace all of me and begin to trust the process. Amen.

"I praise you, for I am fearfully and wonderfully made.[a] Wonderful are your works; my soul knows it very well."
Psalms 139:14

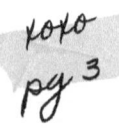
xoxo
pg 3

Your Hearts Reflection

Day 2

I Am Made In His Image

How many of you are daddy's girl? My hand is raised all geeked up because I cherished my Papi. As a daddy's girl, there was something special about being able to physically, emotionally, and mentally connect and know that I was created from this man I called my father. I was in awe of his character, his love for his children (and you wouldn't be able to tell the two that weren't his either), or how he made sure his family never lacked anything. However, when my biological father passed away, I lost that. I was angry with the world and God.

I remember asking God "How could you take the only man who cares about me away?" Baby girl was hurt. Who am I supposed to identify with now?! Who is going to take of care me? He talks trash to me about asking for $5 and still be pulling the wallet out to give. If y'all have Caribbean parents, then you know the struggle to be real. I am glad to let you know that there is a greater Father both you and I can connect our identity to. I am made in His likeness and His image.

Right now, you may be searching for your identity from the loss of a parent, a divorce after 20 years,

xoxo
pg 4

after being everything for everyone and you lost sight of who you are.

I am here to comfort you with the insight of knowing that our identity is connected, made in the image and likeness of someone who is magnificent. That means you are bold, courageous, loving, patient, kind, compassionate, and the list can go on and on. These are the same characteristics that He possesses. Rest assured that your DNA is filled with the blood of power, authority, victory, and dominion. Like Beyoncé said, "Who run the world?" GIRLS. Don't get so caught up in the references and miss the point. For the holier than thou folks: our Father conquered the world and everything in it. So, what does that say about you? Think about it.

Prayer: Daddy, your promise to me is that I was made in your likeness and image, and I need you to reveal that again to me. I know your virtues and I need them to be mine as well. Fully embedded in my DNA, so there's no mistake on my birth certificate. Interject your statues into my vertebrae, so I can stand upright, built with power and authority to exercise my birthright every day of my life. Amen

Scripture:
God created man in his own image, in the image of God he created him; male and female he created them.
Genesis 1:27

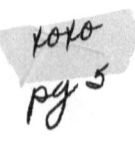

Your Hearts Reflection

Day 3

I Am Set Free

People like to remind us of all the old things we used to do, be, and say. We like to beat ourselves up over past mistakes when we did and didn't know better. As women, we like to overcompensate for our kids, break our backs to right our wrongs, and live with those word curses and make them our truths. Generational curses are not yours to inherit. This stuff is all easier said than done, this I know. The enemy comes to remind us of these things to steal, kill, destroy, and to keep us bound. He comes around like DJ Khaled's, "and another one." Like bruh, how many times do I need the reminder to go off (side eye)?

I was reminded that I was and am free. According to Galatians 1:5, For freedom Christ has set us free; stand firm therefore, and do not submit again to a yoke of slavery. All the bs that the enemy reminds you of is the yoke of slavery because it keeps you bound.

xoxo

pg 6

you're so loved

Do you ever wonder why his broke, disgusted, rejected self tries so hard to keep you off track? Because the moment you really hone into your true power, authority, and birthright, he knows ain't no stopping you now, you're on the move (yes, just start singing the song).

Hand over that old filthy garment and put on your priestly robe and strut your stuff like you would do in a new pair of heels.

Prayer: God, I've been bound by guilt, shame, past mistakes, and condemnation for a long time. You said that I am set free and not held down by this yoke of slavery. I declare this day that I am. I ask for wisdom to deal with the enemy according to every attack and strategy he may bring. Allow me to remain on my post alert, suited and booted, ready for war. God I know that this is not a one-day victory, but you declared that I are more than conquerors, so I will walk in victory daily. Amen.

Scripture:
For freedom Christ has set us free; stand firm therefore, and do not submit again to a yoke of slavery. Galatians 1:5

xoxo
pg 7

Your Hearts Reflection

Day 4

I Am Steadfast

Life trips us up, we fall, and we attempt to get back up. Some of us beat ourselves up down to a plump. Showing no grace, compassion, and mercy for the mistakes you've done years ago. Baby did you just forget how you killed last year, last month, or even last night?

We get so moved and shaken by our circumstances and the imaginary fear that we create about the unthinkable outcome. Shifting ourselves out of alignment not realizing that our identity is what solidifies our connection and existence with our Father.

I AM STEADFAST

2021 has torn down to rebuild in our lives. Circumstances unforeseen. Not only does His word says for me not to be moved but it says that I am steadfast and unmovable.

If you know anything about Christ and His character He wasn't moved by his circumstances, not by people's responses, not by what He saw. If we were him, we probably would've thrown in the towel.

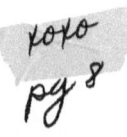

xoxo
pg 8

Remember day one reminded us that we are made in his likeness and image and IF He was unmovable the WE are as well.

What is shaking you in your life that is causing you to step out of the place of steadfastness (firm and unwavering)?

Prayer: Daddy right now _____(insert issue) has gotten my attention however, I refuse to be moved by this situation. Solidify my feet into solid ground where I remain steadfast and unmovable until you move. Amen

Scripture:
Therefore, my beloved brothers, be steadfast, immovable, always abounding in the work of the Lord, knowing that in the Lord your labor is not in vain.
1 Corinthian 15:58

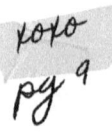
xoxo
pg 9

Your Hearts Reflection

Day 5

I Am A Good Thing

I remember talking to my friend LJ about marriage and my identity as a wife. At this point in my marriage, I felt like scum—the dirt that was beneath his feet. Kids acting a fool and unappreciative of everything. If you know me, I'm good for saying, "I'm about to kick EVERYBODY out." During our conversation, she had to remind me what I brought to the table. This wasn't a bragging session but sometimes we truly do forget how the bomb we truly are. This conversation gave me hope and saved me from a lot of grief.

I am a good thing (Proverbs 18:22) and remind yourself of that every day. I don't care what your status is: a wife, a fiancé, a single woman, a divorcee, remember you are a good thing. Also, because of you, favor is brought into the mix. Girl, if you don't pat yourself on the back and give yourself a hug today, life will test you and make you feel like a total failure.

We'll compare our worth to how well things are going on around us. Home, work, kids, husband, business, when with all due respect, those things have nothing to do with current value or retail price.

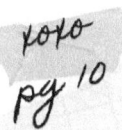

xoxo
pg 10

Matter of fact, you were called to steward over those things, not to compare and contrast. There's no comparison so have several seats, please. Your worth is written on that check from your Father because what He wrote on it will never come back void or returned to the sender.

Prayer: God, I know that I am a good thing because you said I am. However, sometimes I do forget it. I thank you for the Holy Spirit given unto me as a gift that is my advocate and reminder of your word. Allow the Holy Spirit that lives within me to regurgitate your truth when I seem to lose heart and sight of it. Allow every thought to be filtered by your word so I always live-in spirit and in truth. Amen.

Scripture:
He who finds a wife finds what is good and receives favor from the Lord. Proverbs 18:22

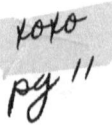
xoxo
pg 11

Your Hearts Reflection

Day 6

I Am Appointed

Did you wake up today realizing how great you are? Did you give yourself credit for how obedient you've been? But for real girl are you allowing that once mistake to keep you away from your destiny and purpose?

I bet you are wondering why you? But the question remains "Aren't you appointed this?" or "Weren't you made to bear fruit among this earth?" Let's be real. Sometimes the doubt creeps in and you go to thinking and believing what the enemy said is true. The results become a stagnant chick with so much potential. God appoints the call not the other way around. He called you and chose you. Not just to be ordinary but appointed and He said go and bear fruit, fruit that it may last.

The result of your birth and walking in your calling will make a lifelong impact in the lives that are connected to you. I bet you don't even realize what's inside of you.
Heck I didn't!

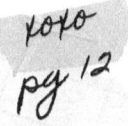

Today is different. YOU ARE APPOINTED! Never doubt that and never allow the enemy to make you believe otherwise.

Prayer: *God you have appointed me to be a steward over the gifts given to me and called me to go and bear fruit. Make clear to me the areas that I am bearing fruit so I can operate in the fullness of my purpose. Amen*

Scripture:
You did not choose me, but I chose you and appointed you so that you might go and bear fruit—fruit that will last—and so that whatever you ask in my name the Father will give you. John 15:16

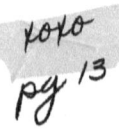

xoxo
pg 13

Your Hearts Reflection

Day 7

I Am Worth More Than Rubies

Diamonds are a girl's best friend. Who lied to us? Everybody. Did you know a 1-carat ruby can out price a 1-carat diamond by double its value? Rubies are made from the mineral corundum or aluminum oxide (yeah, I know, no one came for a science lesson). When rubies are treated to extreme heat and pressure, they are formed under the earth's surface. This means there's no soft piece in that body of yours. Due to the formation and location of rubies, it makes them extremely rare. As I'm giving you this science 101 lesson, I hope you're grasping the characteristics of your uniqueness. The imperfections of the rubies and their color make-up will allow a certified jeweler to know a natural from a lab-created ruby. Scripture says, "She is more precious than rubies; nothing you desire can compare with her."

This means your imperfections make you unique; there's no duplication, you can withstand the extreme heat and pressure of life, worth can't be compared to a single dollar value. So, do me a huge favor right now and adjust the crown that is sitting on your head right now.

xoxo
pg 14

Repeat after me: "I am imperfectly perfect for the calling upon my life. Equipped with all the tools needed to do His will (Hebrews 13:21). And I'm me, no duplicates, just authentically unapologetically me!" Unbeknownst to you, you are talking to the enemy on that note because sometimes you just need to put that clown on notice.

Prayer: Daddy help me to understand that everything is about me is unique. Teach me how to better steward me through my words, actions, and thoughts. Allow me to consider my worth daily with humility and without boast. Please help me never to take my worth for granted. Understanding my worth will allow me to be bolder and bigger, with my faith in turn being a beacon for other women and people connected to me. Let me live this life unapologetically me. Amen.

Scripture:
She is more precious than rubies; nothing you desire can compare with her. Proverbs 3:15

A wife of noble character who can find? She is worth far more than rubies. Proverbs 31:10

Equip you with everything good for doing his will, and may he work in us what is pleasing to him, through Jesus Christ, to whom be glory for ever and ever. Amen.
Hebrews 13:21

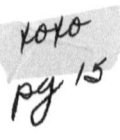

xoxo
pg 15

Your Hearts Reflection

Day 8

I Am Strong And Courageous

You never know what you are made of until you are put in the fire. I know we all have our own individual stories and what I also know is that it may resemble the fire experienced by the three Hebrews boys. One thing that the fire taught you is how to be strong. You didn't know you could be a single mother, a divorcee, or even a strong wife. Let's not get it twisted; married women need strength too. Cause honey, it takes a lot to be humble and bite ya tongue when you really want to say a few choice words of your own. But God gives us the strength to be courageous, to live in spirit and truth, to operate out of boldness, and to learn how to be authentically you. It takes strength to do that and more.

It took strength to walk out on faith when others doubted you or counted you out. When family and friends alienated you because you chose to go against the grain, take a step back and really look at yourself and how far you've come. Just sigh and smile because you overcame a lot.

xoxo
pg 16

Take a moment to reflect because you probably haven't even given yourself time to do so. I'm telling you I'm proud of you. God is proud of you. Now it is time for you to be proud of you. Life could have taken you right out but, you stood with courage.

If you lack strength and want to have more courage, did you know all you had to do is just ask? So, let's do so:

Prayer: Father God, I need your grace that is sufficient to meet me in this place. I want to have the strength to face my fears, the courage to walk by faith, and the courage to never look back. Allow my strength to be your strength because I know I cannot do this on my own. You said if we lack anything, all we had to do is ask, so today I am asking for more _____. With the measure of faith that I have, let me move and continue to build with every step that I take. I will not fret for you are with me wherever I go. Let this measure be shut up in my bones that I won't second guess or be hesitant to follow your instructions. Amen.

Scripture:
Have I not commanded you? Be strong and courageous. Do not be frightened, and do not be dismayed, for the Lord your God is with you wherever you go. Joshua 1:9

Your Hearts Reflection

Day 9

I Am Chosen

Have you ever felt like everyone around you was getting blessed and you started to wonder and ask God "Uhmmmm, so you said you are not a respective of person but yet why does it seem like everybody is getting blessed but me?" (Confused face). God said He chose you for the calling upon your life. The assignment that He put you on for His glory to be met.

Do you know that sometimes our biggest barrier is our belief in knowing that HE CHOSE US? He chose you for that assignment, He chose you for that business, for that profession, for that career, for that ministry, for that family, and for the legacy that you will leave behind. He chose you once He wrote your name down in that book of life.

Say this out loud, "I am chosen for such a time as this!" What reflects "such a time" for you right now? Do you even believe that it's yours? Side eye. Learn how to bet on yourself for once. I mean really, what do you have to lose?

xoxo
pg 18

NOTHING!! Knowing this allows you to experience His best every day. Isn't that what you desire?

Prayer: God, you chose me and called me by name. My imperfections and insecurities you know them all; however, you still choose to pursue me every day. I was chosen from my mother's womb; I was chosen even when I sinned and went against your name. You still chose me. There is nothing missing nor broken in my life because I am chosen. I lack no good thing because I am chosen. I experience you best because I am chosen. I have favor with both you and man because I am chosen. The enemy flees when He sees me because I am chosen. God allow me to see the power behind being a chosen vessel and let me not take it for granted. Amen.

Scripture:
You did not choose me, but I chose you. Jn 15:16.

Even as he chose us in him before the foundation of the world, that we should be holy and blameless before him. Ephesians 1:4

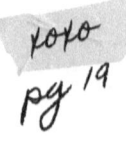
xoxo
pg 19

Your Hearts Reflection

Day 10

I Am Stable In All My Ways

Yeah, yeah, yeah, blame it on the Libra's: y'all the most indecisive people I know. But the reality is we deal with that spirit when we lack trust in the Holy Spirit that works within us. We struggle because we don't trust God and halfway be thinking that we can handle it on our own. The battle is because your flesh and spirit have two different desires and now, we have an issue. That's the fight you on-site battle. Please don't act like I'm the only one who was on that time type of time. The key to stability is having confidence and faith in knowing who God is and the power He has in and over your life. Being stable means that you are firmly fixed, no deviation. Let's journey back to being a daddy's girl for a second.

Do you remember your daddy making you a promise, saying he'll get you something or do something for you? Do you also remember talking trash to your friends in school "Yes, uh MY DADDY SAID he promised he's going to get that for me!" Then walking away mad because they just tried you and your daddy. It didn't matter what came out of your father's mouth if HE said it, your heart was settled and at ease. There was no internal battle.

xoxo

pg 20

Now imagine being that confident in the God you serve. Your flesh and spirit man must line up in return, causing no fluctuation in your decisions, actions, speech, and the boss girl moves. This will bring a stability in your life that even when the enemy comes with his tired tactics, it will be an easy shutdown.

Prayer: Daddy, I decree and declare that I am not a double-minded man, but I am stable in all my emotions, my thoughts, my temperament, my actions, my reactions, and my decisions that need to be made. I will not vacillate but will trust and have confidence in you that you will lead and guide me accordingly along this journey. Allow me to be firmly fixed, not battling between flesh and spirit but my flesh will become submissive to your spirit. Amen.

Scripture:
But let him ask in faith, with no doubting, for the one who doubts is like a wave of the sea that is driven and tossed by the wind. 7 For that person must not suppose that he will receive anything from the Lord; 8 he is a double-minded man, unstable in all his ways. James 1:6-8

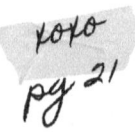

xoxo
pg 21

Your Hearts Reflection

Day 11
I Cannot Fall/Fail

If failing was not an option, where would you be right now? How much would you have accomplished? We may think about or these ask questions when we find ourselves in a rut. I'm here screaming failing is not an option. There may be delays, moments where you will have to wait, and those L's that you thought you took were exposures and lessons to be learned for the bigger blessing. The book of life reminds us that God conquered the world, which makes our obstacles different. Man, I am soooo speaking to myself right now. I can't fall or fail, and neither can you. In times of trouble, He promised to save us at the break of day.

It's one thing to read the word but, it is another thing to actually believe that they are applicable to your life. He is on your side, your biggest cheerleader. He's saying I got you, just believe that I do. I won't leave you nor forsake you, I won't harm you but give you an expected end. The process may not feel good but, I will be with you wherever you go, even if you make your bed in hell, I'm there. What more of a commitment do you need? We take the sweet nothings that a man whisper and fall head over heels but can't take His word for face value. Come on!

xoxo
pg 22

Prayer: Daddy, let me know that I can do anything with your strength and there is no failing in you. I may stumble but I will not fall and when I am in trouble, you will save me. Let that truly resonate with me until it becomes second nature to me. I know you're in my corner and I know you're my biggest cheerleader but, sometimes doubt creeps in and try to throw me off my game. However, I will no longer believe the lie of the enemy. I can make it and I shall succeed. There's no failure in me because there is no failure in you. Amen.

Scripture:
God is within her; she will not fall; God will help her at break of day. Psalm 46:5

Your Hearts Reflection

Day 12
I Am Appointed

Before you were born, know that you were chosen and set apart. Do you wonder why sometimes it feels like you don't fit in certain places, groups, or social gatherings? Fitting in brings in the feeling of being comfortable. He keeps you in a state of un-comfortability because there are some things you need to birth, some generational curses you need to break, word curses you need to rebuke. You were appointed a seat to go and bear fruit, especially with your name on it.

Your seat has power. It gives you the authority to bear fruit and that your fruit will be long lasting. This means your fruit with a generational, bloodline inheritance, so it does not start and end with you. We are talking legacies.

Your appointed seat gives you the birthright to ask your Father anything in His name and it is yours. Girl, what more can you ask for? We are comfortable being appointed because it's your birthright, now use it.

xoxo
pg 24

Prayer: Father, I was thought about, written about, and created with this appointment to be set apart from the rest. You called me to bear good fruit that will carry on through my lineage. Let me take full authority, accountability, and ownership of my birthright. My journey will not fall short of your glory. Amen.

Scripture:
You did not choose me, but I chose you and appointed you that you should go and bear fruit and that your fruit should abide, so that whatever you ask the Father in my name, he may give it to you. John 15:16

Your Hearts Reflection

Day 13

I Am Made Beautiful

I was a diamond in a rough. For those that don't know what that means, it means one having exceptional qualities or potential but lacking refinement or polish. Being born His child, I had some amazing qualities. I was smart, beautiful, had a smile that would lift hearts, loyal, trustworthy, etc., but all that meant nothing because I didn't know how to really utilize the gifts that were given to me as a woman. Refinement of diamonds starts off as a dirty process; however, with time, pressure, and fire, it becomes a jewel many kill for, risk their life to embezzle. The most important piece in the process of polishing a diamond is the bruiting step. In this step, the diamond is shaped into a specific cut. This process is the most intensive and takes the most time to perfect. So why rush your process?

Your journey doesn't determine your outcome or your destination. You may not be all polished like YOU would like to be, your life may not have been all peaches and cream, and you may be going through your transformation right now. I am here to confirm that it will be life-changing, breath-taking, and amazing when God is done with you. No matter what you are going through.

you're so loved

xoxo

pg 26

trust the process. He makes everything beautiful in His timing. Like the book of Ecclesiastes chapter 3 reminds us that there is a time for everything, and your time is now.

Embrace the process and get excited for the woman you won't recognize.

Prayer: God, there has been a pressing in my spirit, and I cannot even begin to process this. You make everything beautiful in its timing and I thank you for choosing me. You chose me to beautify, to refine, to chisel all the impurities that stand in the way, and I want to say thank you. Let me submit without question and embrace every moment of this process. Protect my heart, mind, and emotions as you keep me close. Amen.

Scripture:
He has made everything beautiful in its time. Ecclesiastes 3:11

Behold, you are beautiful, my love, behold, you are beautiful! Solomon 4:1

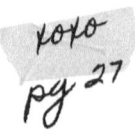

Your Hearts Reflection

Day 14

I Am The Light

You ever felt like you were suffocating in your own skin. The inner you is screaming, "LET ME OUT!" With nowhere to go because you have been hiding her and keeping her hidden from the world. Afraid of what people may think or feel about who you truly are. Have you dimmed your light so that people will feel comfortable? Or have you dimmed your light so that you won't ruffle the wrong feathers?

Get out of your head and emotions. Stop dimming your light for other people when you were given that light to shine before others. To give God the glory that He deserves. To show the world that the good, bad, ugly, and in-between means that you are human and that you are called for a purpose. Let your light shine. Your light will give other people hope to make it another day. Allowing other women like me, you, and us to know that it is okay to be vulnerable without judgement, ridicule, or being looked at less than. Like Rhianna says, Shine bright like a diamond.

xoxo

pg 28

Prayer: Daddy, I may not understand the extent of the goodness that lies within me. The power of my light, my gifts, my anointing, and truly my calling. However, each day allows me to see more and more how I am a blessing to others. Let me now dim your light by the response of man but allow me to grow more confident with every move of faith. You said I am a Beacon, and I will lead others and you lead me. AMEN.

Scripture:
Let your light shine before others Matthew 5:16

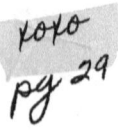
xoxo
pg 29

Your Hearts Reflection

Day 15

I Am Restored

I'm singing "We got London on the track." Just kidding, just kidding. I am singing this oldie, "When my journey weighs on me, He restores." Have you ever been broken, in a place of despair, confused, tired of being sick and tired, and just flat out desperate? Some of us have been through the roller-coaster of being betrayed, lie to and on, abused, alienated, counted out, and dropped by the person that meant the most to us? Do you remember those feelings like you couldn't go on another day? Trying to figure out what the next move is going to be or telling yourself, "My comeback game is gonna be strong and they gonna feel me." All that was good and dandy but when it got silent, you're in bed at night, and can't sleep, EVERYTHING came back like a rushing wind, overwhelming to say the least.

God is a restorer and a redeemer of all things. Time, energy, finances, emotions, and heart like you never missed a beat. Learning how to place all things in His hands is sometimes the biggest battle. Only picking and choosing what we want to give him to restore but He is saying, "I got you." I will restore the broken places in your heart; I will restore your soul, I will restore what you thought you lost in the deal, I WILL RESTORE.

xoxo

pg 30

*Prayer: God, I've been through some things. Some I acknowledge and some I continue to suppress but, I am asking you to bring down the rain and let it shower on my life. That way all the things unaddressed, suppressed, and oppressed would surface to the top so we can address them together. I need to be restored and renewed from the pain, guilt, shame, resentment, and unforgiveness that lies within me. Restore my soul oh God, like you know best. I want to be made whole that nothing is missing, nothing is broken in my life. Take me as I am today, search my heart, and make me new.
Amen.*

Scripture:
He restores my soul. Psalm 23:3

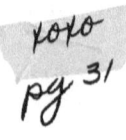

xoxo
pg 31

Your Hearts Reflection

Day 16
I Can Do All Things

In 2017, I graduated from graduate school. I went to school to obtain my nurse practitioner's license. In 2018, I attempted that exam twice and failed both times. The first exam by 9 points, the second by 4 points. I was devasted. I cried and threw away my nursing books, lab coat, and study material. My failure was heartbreaking. My third attempt came in 2019, failed again! I got deployed in 2020 for COVID with the Navy and things went south. I was depressed from the isolation and separation of my family. Heartbroken from all the patients that had lost hope in their eyes and felt like we were the dumping ground for death. "God, my God, where are you?" I asked.

He responded, "I am right here." Once I removed the obstacles out of my view and kept God in the forefront, He began to show me that I could do all things by and with His strength. He started giving me coping skills in my alone time, giving me guidance on how to pray over my patients, and even how to start studying. His strength fed my soul daily and it moved me. That strength kept me sane, it kept me alive, and it made me victorious. I came home and sought counseling, I came home and passed my exam, I came home, and my priorities changed.

xoxo
pg 32

Let us pray.

Prayer: God, I need your strength for my current situation. I am struggling with _____ and you are the only one that can provide a way out. I'm calling you. Not my bestie, not my parents, but you. The Way Maker, my Provider, my Prince of peace, and my Avenger. Your word promises me that I can do all things through your strength. It even affirms that greater is He that exists in me than he that exists in the world, so God I need your strength. I need your power to get me through this. I can't make it or do this on my own, so that's why I am reaching out to you in my most vulnerable place. If it's not going to pass me by, then keep me and allow me to continue to press. Be with me and continue to strengthen me. Amen.

Scripture:
I can do all things through him who strengthens me.
Philippians 4:13

xoxo
pg 33

Your Hearts Reflection

Day 17
I Am Free From Condemnation

People often like to remind you of the old you as if you forgot. Ma'am/Sir, I remember frankly what kind of heathen I was. Those conversations trigger a lot of unsettled emotions, spoken words, hurtful events, and darkness that suppresses your today. It doesn't matter how changed you are, some people like to keep you boxed in their space of limitation. Certain nicknames are associated with your past self that further secludes you in that cage of bondage.

You are free of condemnation. Condemnation is a very strong sense of disapproval or a cruel sense of punishment of sentencing. For each day you remain in the past allows the words spoken over your life to be a constant meditation, or continues to open the door for other people's limitations to prevent you from living and flourishing; this is a sentence from hell. God has set you free and where He is there is freedom. Make that declaration over your life right now. I AM FREE FROM CONDEMNATION. No more will you remember those moments as if that is who you are today, reject and rebuke when people bring up the past, and definitely remind yourself that you are no longer her.

xoxo
pg 34

One more thing, stop feeling guilty about being a newer version of yourself. You are acting funny. You think you brand new? Chile, ever since she xyz, she doesn't come around anymore. Who the heck cares? Make the decisions that are best for you and your freedom in Christ. Bye Felicia and find somebody else to play with cause I am not the one.

Prayer: Daddy, I thank you for the mind of reflection and I rebuke the spirit of condemnation over my life. I come against every word spoken, word prayed, people's limitations, and their remembrance of who I used to be. I thank you for the new creature that I am today. I thank you that I have found you and because I did, I am set free from bondage and condemnation. This battle won't be a one and done but I thank you for defending and delivering me every time. Let my mind rest in Christ Jesus. Amen.

Scripture:
There is therefore now no condemnation for those who are in Christ Jesus. Romans 8:1

xoxo
pg 35

Your Hearts Reflection

Day 18

I Am Royalty

Crown me and let me take my rightful place because I am a part of a royal priesthood. When you think of "someone of royal status," what do you think of? There's no easy access to them, they have endless resources, they have a different posture because they know what they are worth, and they have power. So, ma'am, take a moment to examine what you think and exhibit about your royal priesthood status.

Do you give dogs what is holy or give your precious pearls to pigs? (Matthew 7:6) We give people statuses and ranks where it is unwarranted, PERIODT. From relationships, friendships, associates, and whatever else you want to call them. Know and walk out this journey like you are a chosen generation, a royal priesthood, a holy nation, and God's possession. God has never allowed any of His possession to go to waste or be unvalued. So why would He let someone or something devalue you? And this goes for you too. The price tag that someone places on you is the one you let them. Understand that you are royalty. I'm not saying go out there holding your nose in the air but, what I am saying is understand your birthright. You were meant to demonstrate the marvelous things of God.

xoxo
pg 36

Prayer: God, you said that I am a chosen generation, a royal priesthood, a holy nation, and called to your possession and I thank you for picking me every single day. Help me to understand the fullness of my birthright and lineage by your bloodline. Let me not continue to give my precious pearls to swine to trample and devalue your masterpiece. Guide me as I walk with prestige and excellence in every area of my life. Father God, you have an enduring plan for the chosen to serve with your excellencies among this earth for the kingdom and I won't take this charge lightly. Amen.

Scripture:
But you are a chosen race, aa royal priesthood, a holy nation, a people for his own possession, that you may proclaim the excellencies of him who called you out of darkness into this marvelous light. 1 Peter 2:9

xoxo
pg 37

Your Hearts Reflection

Day 19

I Am More Than Conquerors

To be more than conqueror means that you are victorious over an adversary, trial, or tribulation. God's version of you being more than conqueror is experiencing an overpowering sense of victories not just one. Look at the text, Romans 8:37 "No, in all these things we are more than conquerors through him who loved us." It said "more than conquerors" not more than a conqueror. Huge difference. That's a plural meaning. You're not just going to conquer one obstacle but many. In addition, it says in all things you will be more than conquerors, double confirmation of the context. God already conquered or subdued the world, so what does that mean for you?

What obstacle or mountain are you facing right now that you feel like you can't win? God does miraculous things for His children. Do you remember that situation that you thought you would never overcome, yeah that one? Can I ask you to recall how God showed up on time? Stand firm in your faith, knowing that trouble won't last always, and you are more than conqueror.

xoxo
pg 38

Prayer: Father God, I know the true enemy is Satan. He brings the joy-stealing, destiny-killing, and malicious attack to take me out. However, today I know and understand that I am more than conqueror. I will continue to have faith when I may feel like there is no faith. Allow my spirit to rest in knowing that I am a conqueror, and I will experience your overwhelming experiences of many victories. Amen.

Scripture:
No, in all these things we are more than conquerors through him who loved us. Romans 8:37

xoxo
pg 39

Your Hearts Reflection

Day 20

I Am A Masterpiece

When referring to someone's masterpiece, we are referring to a work of outstanding or excellent artistry, skillset, or product of creation. The level of skill that was imparted in their work demonstrates their workmanship. The word masterpiece places emphasis on the creation. In Ephesians 2:10, other words are used, such as workmanship. The connection between workmanship is where the credit is given. The emphasis on masterpiece is placed on you. Your creation and the time that was dedicated to creating you. The impartation behind the vision and heart of the workman. Workmen give credit to God, the creator.

When you look at yourself in the mirror, what do you see? A masterpiece or a common work of art? Everything that God create is of value. He formed us in the way He wanted and would bring pleasure and purpose for His Kingdom. He utilized the tools of relationships, adversaries, miracles, and challenges to chisel away the things that need to be removed from your life.

xoxo

pg 40

He reminds us that He is the gardener, and He promises to finish the good work He began in you (Philippians 1:6).

Prayer: Daddy, allow me to fall in love with your masterpiece. I am your creation filled with your virtues to filled with the capacity to carry the vision. You will complete the good work you've started within me. You will not allow any unfinished work to be birthed out of my life. I am your responsibility, so as you look after the bird, you cover me at a greater level. Let me be patient with the process, knowing it will produce faith, endurance, and perseverance. Amen.

Scripture:
For we are God's masterpiece. Ephesians 2:10 (NLT)

And I am sure of this, that he who began a good work in you will bring it to completion at the day of Jesus Christ.
Philippians 1:6

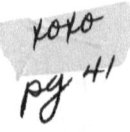
xoxo
pg 41

Your Hearts Reflection

Day 21

I Am Blessed

How you are you doing this morning? Blessed and highly favored. We say these phrases without understanding or believing the impact behind them. Deuteronomy 28:1-14 tell you how blessed you really are. It says He will set you high above all the nations of the earth. All blessings shall come upon you and overtake you. Have you ever been overtaken by something? That means you have no control over the extent of these blessings to come. In these scriptures, God uses the word shall. Shall means that there is an instruction or command that God is giving. It also means that there is a great assertion that it will happen. There is intent to these commands on instruction for your life.

You are truly blessed and highly favored. God reminds us that we have favor with both Him and man (Proverbs 3:4). Embrace this. Stop walking around here like there's no power, anointing, favor, blessings connected to you. God will give you the measure of grace to walk out His purpose over your life. It's a blessing to be a blessing and that you are.

xoxo
pg 42

Prayer: Daddy, let your blessings overtake me and consume me. Let there be a fresh wind that blows over me today that refreshes my soul into knowing the capacity of my anointing in you. Your word asserts that everything you say concerning me is not a wish list but a definite command to the four corners of this earth that shall become obedient because you spoke a thing. So I thank you today, Daddy, for allowing me to have favor with both you and man. Thank you for allowing me to be blessed coming in and blessed coming out. My first fruits are blessed, my family is blessed, my finances are blessed, my business(es) are blessed. You over see everything that concerns me, so there's no lack or deficient. I will forever be a blessing to your kingdom. Amen.

Scripture:
And if you faithfully obey the voice of the Lord your God, being careful to do all his commandments that I command you today, the Lord your God will set you high above all the nations of the earth. 2 And all these blessings shall come upon you and overtake you, if you obey the voice of the Lord your God. 3 Blessed shall you be in the city and blessed shall you be in the field. 4 Blessed shall be the fruit of your womb and the fruit of your ground and the fruit of your cattle, the increase of your herds and the young of your flock. 5 Blessed shall be your basket and your kneading bowl.

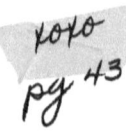
xoxo
pg 43

6 Blessed shall you be when you come in and blessed shall you be when you go out. 7 "The Lord will cause your enemies who rise against you to be defeated before you. They shall come out against you one way and flee before you seven ways. 8 The Lord will command the blessing on you in your barns and in all that you undertake. And he will bless you in the land that the Lord your God is giving you. 9 The Lord will establish you as a people holy to himself, as he has sworn to you, if you keep the commandments of the Lord your God and walk in his ways. 10 And all the peoples of the earth shall see that you are called by the name of the Lord, and they shall be afraid of you. 11 And the Lord will make you abound in prosperity, in the fruit of your womb and in the fruit of your livestock and in the fruit of your ground, within the land that the Lord swore to your fathers to give you. 12 The Lord will open to you his good treasury, the heavens, to give the rain to your land in its season and to bless all the work of your hands. And you shall lend to many nations, but you shall not borrow. 13 And the Lord will make you the head and not the tail, and you shall only go up and not down, if you obey the commandments of the Lord your God, which I command you today, being careful to do them, 14 and if you do not turn aside from any of the words that I command you today, to the right hand or to the left, to go after other gods to serve them.
Exodus 28:1-14

xoxo
pg 44

So you will find favor and good success[a] in the sight of God and man. Proverbs 3:4

xoxo

pg 45

Your Hearts Reflection

Day 22

I Am Not Afraid

Did you know that we are reminded 365 times not to be afraid in the Bible? Yep, look it up. God is so comical that He already knew that my daughters are going to need a daily reminder of my commandment. It appears as: don't fret, fear not, do not be afraid, etc., 365 times. Fear is a false preconcerted illusion created by you without the experience of its reality. You made this whole scenario, picture, conversation, and outcome in your mind before even doing anything. The result becomes an abandoned dream, an un-birthed vision, or a dropped purpose.

What's so crazy is that when we do finally muster up the courage to do it, you ask yourself, "What was I so afraid of? It wasn't that bad." Sounds very familiar, huh? I know because I've done it. I've talked myself out of opportunities that were aligned just for me. Here's another question that even God asks us, "What can man do you?" Do you trust God? Do you believe that He got you against all odds? That He will never leave you nor forsake you?

xoxo
pg 46

Make the choice today to stop living in fear. Walk boldly in everything you do, everything you say, and everything you think because God is there with you, leading you every day. Fear not.

Prayer: Father God, fear comes and sometimes tries to choke the life out of me like the python spirit and I bind up every emotion associated with fear, all old experiences, the fear of the response of man, and whatever else that I am unaware of that keeps me bound. I break every chain and shackle and I loose boldness, confidence, and courage into my life. Man cannot stop me on my tracks to victory and purpose so let my soul be not afraid. Let me trust you at a greater level. Increase my capacity of faith to take every needed step. Let me trust my thoughts, for they are your thoughts and my ways your ways. I command fear to flee from me this day. Amen.

Scripture:
So we can confidently say, "The Lord is my helper; I will not fear; what can man do to me?" Hebrews 13:6

The Lord is on my side; I will not fear. What can man do to me? Psalm 118:6

In God, whose word I praise, in God I trust; I shall not be afraid. What can flesh do to me? Psalm 56:4

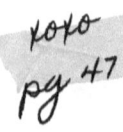

xoxo
pg 47

Your Hearts Reflection

Day 23

I Am Confident

You ever got dressed, make-up beaten, hair done, and eyebrows slayed? That made you want to sing like Beyonce, "I'm a grown woman, I do whatever I want", start doing that African choreography, sling your hair, and walk out the door like aye. There's an igniting fire that consumes you. No one in their right mind would have the courage to tell you anything less. What if you can experience that confidence every day? What if that could be a daily routine instead of a couple of times a year?

Through you surrendering and allowing God to finish the good work He started in you, will be long-lived. You will wake up every morning rest assured in the confidence and power of the God you pray to, the God you talk about, the God that you serve. This kind of confidence allows you to trust God in the good times, bad times, and ugly times. Remain confident that He will do what He promised, but you must know what He said to stand on that promise. Have you asked Him lately?

xoxo
pg 48

Prayer: God, I desire a daily dose of your confidence to be a part of my DNA. I want my blood to be enriched not fortified and altered but just pure enrichment of confidence. Sometimes I am not confident because of fear, lack of faith, lack of trust, and lack of belief in your capability to do a thing. Today, I'm asking you to help me in my unbelief. I can't walk in confidence with this fearful posture, so I need you to search, expose, and rid me of this. I choose to walk with my head held high, knowing that you complete this good work, your purpose, your divine will for my life, and that I am confident of. Amen.

Scripture:

Being confident of this, that he who began a good work in you will carry it on to completion until the day of Christ Jesus. Philippians 1:6

In the fear of the Lord one has strong confidence, and his children will have a refuge. Proverbs 14:26

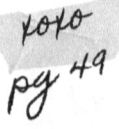

xoxo
pg 49

Your Hearts Reflection

_____

_____

_____

_____

_____

_____

_____

_____

_____

_____

_____

_____

_____

Day 24

I Am Bold As A Lion

Lions are spoken about in reference to their power and courage. They are legendary for their fearlessness. As believers, this is something that we naturally inherit but don't operate in. Lions are lean in stature with little to no fat, well-muscled and toned. This insinuates that we ladies need to get rid of all the excess baggage that keeps us weighed down. When a lion comes into the scene, all other animals and living human beings flee because of the known damage that this one animal could do. Other creatures that are 10 times the height and weight of a lion remain full of fear. Why isn't the enemy and the atmosphere running when they see you? Do you lack power, courage, and commitment? God said if we lack anything, we could and should ask and He will give it generously (James 1:5).

Ask yourself what it would take for you to be bold as lion and begin to petition that before you Heavenly Father. He's waiting on you, He's waiting to hear your hearts cry and desire.

you're so loved

xoxo

pg 50

Prayer: Daddy, my spiritual composition needs refining. I want to be lean, powerful, and full of courage. I need the transformation taking place on the inside of me to reflect in my natural life as well. I want to be an atmospheric changer, enemy slayer, and burst hell wide open by the strength that lies within me. When I open my mouth and speak, it will be like a roar that shakes things up, correct things, places things back in order. My only request is that you teach me how to do all this with love and humility. Remove all the prideful areas and let me remain meek before you. Amen.

Scripture:
But the righteous are bold as a lion. Proverbs 28:1

xoxo
pg 51

Your Hearts Reflection

Day 25

I Am Never Alone

I've had days, nights, and even mid-day tears of feeling like I was so alone. Crying out to God and felt like He gave me the deuces sign. This place started to be filled with darkness because I started disconnecting myself from people and being anti-social. This caused me to seclude myself from fellowship and just hanging out and having a good time. God had to check me one day and put me in my place. Those nights you paced the floor, He said I was there. When you sat in your car and cried your make-up off, He said I was there. When you felt unsatisfied with life and wanted to throw in the towel, He said I was there. When you attempted to commit suicide, He said I was there.

We are never alone. We may feel lonely at times, but God promises us that we are never alone. He will never leave us or forsake us (Hebrews 13:5). He assures us that He will be with us always (Matthew 28:20). He said I will help you, I will strengthen you, and I will uphold you (Isaiah 41:10).

xoxo

pg 52

In addition, God places people in your life that truly fight for you in the spirit. The enemy attempts to make us feel like we are alone because there is power in number. The prayers of the righteous availeth much. Don't allow your angels to go into solo, he/she need backup. Send them into battle with an army.

Prayer: God, I know I am not ever alone. In those moments when I start to feel that embrace me with your arms and keep me close. Allow me to rest in your bosoms and presence until I am comforted. You said you are with me, leading me and guiding me, allowing your words to light up my pathway. I am truly never alone. Daddy, I need you and I want you to know that I am nothing without you. Let me dwell in that secret place until I am full and my cup runneth over with your certainty. I take your hand and will never let it go. Amen.

Scripture:
And behold, I am with you always, to the end of the age.
Matthew 28:20

xoxo
pg 53

Your Hearts Reflection

Day 26
I Am Accepted

The pain of rejection will cause you to go in a place of desperation and become a motivator to do things that you would have never done—going the extra mile to prevent that pain from ever being relived. The rejection experienced while being a wife was mortifying. I gave myself one of those "never again pep talks" because I never wanted to feel that pain ever and even to allow someone that much power over my emotions.

The reality is and was that my acceptance could only be validated and come from Christ Jesus. People will reject you because we are human and we reject what makes us feel uncomfortable, threatened, misunderstood, etc. But Jesus will never reject you, make you unworthy, less than, not qualified for and that is all that matters. Come as you are; you don't need to put on your Sunday's best.

xoxo
pg 54

Prayer: Father God, thank you for taking me as I am. Let not the hurt of rejection drive me away from you; however, allow it to bring me closer. As I draw near, heal me, restore me, and renew me. I know that I am accepted and covered by your blood. Amen.

Scripture:
For if their rejection means the reconciliation of the world, what will their acceptance mean but life from the dead? Romans 11:15

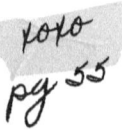
xoxo
pg 55

Your Hearts Reflection

Day 27

I Am Not Here To Please Man

Social media has been a blessing and the death of us. The likes, comments, and views have all laid an impression of our worth to the point we change ourselves to please the people. We become co-dependent on being liked by others, changing who we are to fit the status quo. Resulting in us to gear our actions, word, and decisions to what they would like or approve of. This is the motivational force that drives people to make decisions based on the false approval they believe they will receive.

People-pleasing will take you on a down-hill spiral to doom. We cannot serve two masters; our intent should be to please God. It was commanded to us that we owe no man nothing. Instead of seeking validation, solidification, and approval from people who don't really matter, try seeking it from the person who already had an expected end for your life—the one who knows the blueprint. The same man that can heal, restore, and redeem what you've lost.

xoxo
pg 56

Prayer: God, I'm tired of seeking ways to please people. It has not added any more value to my life. I want to please you for everything I need comes from you. Let me not become dependent on the likes, praises, and comments of others but let me be free in you to please you. Amen

Scripture:
For am I now seeking the approval of man, or of God? Or am I trying to please man? If I were still trying to please man, I would not be a servant of Christ. Galatians 1:10

xoxo
pg 57

Your Hearts Reflection

Day 28
I Am Walking By Faith

Life is a faith walk. Faith is the total confidence in something or someone. Every day we have a decision to make on who we are going to trust and the execution of that decision. Faith is also defined as things that we hope for, evidence of things unseen. God wants us to be able to walk in blind faith. That no matter what the situation may look like, you are betting on God to deliver. You are believing in restoration. You are believing in that breakthrough. This looks like letting go of the way you usually did or do things and allowing God to take the wheel. Not just at half the wheel but completely letting go and trusting Him with your life. Our issue is that we like to pick and choose what areas we want to walk by faith. That is not the mandate.

There are women in the bible who left everything behind to follow Jesus and the word of the Lord. Chile, I commend them, and I too, want to be just like them, total faith. Walking by faith and not what's in front of me. Having the faith of a mustard seed that will move these mountains. Faith that all things will work out for my good because I love the Lord.

xoxo
pg 58

It's a foolish (or unwise) tactic to try and succeed on flesh or human efforts alone. There is an open invitation to experience the supernatural with God. The miracles, signs, and wonders that He is ready to expose you and give you a taste. Come out of your comfort zone and enlarge your territory. You can't do this alone.

Prayer: Father God, I am tired of doing things my way. When I put my hands in the pot, I mess it all up and I repent now. I submit to walking in blind faith, oh God, knowing that everything will work out for my good. I have excluded you and trusted myself more than I have your power. Allow me to believe in your limitless, undeniable abilities and what can be done in my life if I only surrender. Amen
Scripture:

Are you so foolish? After beginning by means of the Spirit, are you now trying to finish by means of the flesh? Galatians 3:3

Now faith is the assurance of things hoped for, the conviction of things not seen. Hebrews 11:1

xoxo
pg 59

Your Hearts Reflection

Day 29

I Am Predestined

Walking in purpose should not be a dreaded, never-finding process. God wants to provide you with the insight needed and wisdom to understand your purpose. This will allow you to walk with boldness and confidence in your lane. I know this journey has not been easy, but please understand that every bump in the road and every happenstance all plays an important role.

It is easy to think that you are disqualified for the job, the role, motherhood, being a wife, that promotion, that business, that house, and the call. God came to remind you that He predestined you when He called you. Your life was crafted just for you to walk in, so stop cutting yourself short. You were built Jesus tough. You are hand-selected, not a number picked out of a box. Handcrafted to His perfection. My God.

Prayer: Lord, help me to give myself more grace when I mess up or fall short. Let me find joy and purpose in my imperfections, knowing that the outcome will lead to your perfection.

xoxo

pg 60

I am predestined for this journey and let me count it all joy when it doesn't feel or look good. Mature me where I am immature and let me put all my childish ways aside. You promised that you lead me and instruct me, so I will never go astray. I am equipped with everything that I need. Amen.

Scripture:
And those whom he predestined he also called, and those whom he called he also justified, and those whom he justified he also glorified. Romans 8:30

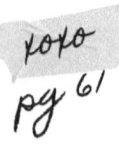

Your Hearts Reflection

Day 30

I Am Embracing All Of Me

"Let's just go ahead and be what we were made to be, without enviously or pridefully comparing ourselves with each other, or trying to be something we aren't" Romans 12:6-7 (MSG). I could drop the mic right here and walk off stage but I'm not going to do that. This is a pure statement in which we all struggle with. God made us individually, imperfectly, perfect just the way we are, there are no duplicates and I've said this before.

This world has shaped the way we think, feel, and move through their demands. This scripture provides us with the confidence and glimpse of what God wants us to do, "go ahead and be what we were made to be." He gave us permission do to so, who gon' check ya boo? NOBODY. Now take the opportunity to embrace that full, slim, or thick future and embrace that you will not fit in with everyone. Embrace that your vision sounds too good to be naturally true because God is going to make it supernaturally possible. Embrace that you are appointed, that you have power, and dominion, and favor.

xoxo
pg 62

Going through the journey requires you to embrace who you are and be authentically you. That is what people will fall in love with, the grace that is given unto you to be you.

Prayer: God, allow me to trust and embrace the uniqueness of your creation which is me. You've formed me the way I am because it is pleasing to you—my personality, voice, attitude, body make up, and individuality. Let me not take these things for granted nor misuse them. You've designed me so fearlessly, beautifully, wonderfully, and strategically all for your glory. Amen.

Scripture:
Let's just go ahead and be what we were made to be, without enviously or pridefully comparing ourselves with each other, or trying to be something we aren't. Romans 12: 6-7 MSG

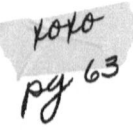
xoxo
pg 63

Your Hearts Reflection

_____

_____

_____

_____

_____

_____

_____

_____

_____

_____

_____

_____

_____

Bonus

I Am Who I Think I Am

So a man thinketh so is he (Proverbs 23:7). What is the meditation on your heart and mind about who you are? We've gone through 29 days of going over what God said, how He views you, and the masterpiece behind His creation. Today I want you to write some new declarations, new beliefs, and new tactics because now that you are proclaiming God's doing a new thing in you, he will test you. Start looking for different results in your life. Henry Ford also said, "Whether you think you can, or you think you can't--you're right."

The limitations of your life comes from your belief system. It's time to do a system check. Ask for what you're lacking, be honest about where you are so He can get you to where you need to be. Check your thoughts and make sure they align with His truth. Cut the enemy off at the zero-yard line; please allow no running plays.

xoxo
pg 64

Prayer: God, I've had some altered visions about who I am. Through these 29 days, I've had the opportunity to read what you called me to be, do, think, and believe. Remove the scales from my eyes and let me see with your lenses. Let the meditation of my mind and heart be pleasing unto you. Let me run with the vision as you make it plain. I am bold and courageous. Called and appointed to do your divine will. My mind is sound that I only hear your thoughts and voice. Renew me today, search me today, and make me white as snow. I remove my old garment and put on my new garment of praise, for I am excited about what's to come. I totally surrender my agenda, time stamps on life, and plans to be subjective to the plans you have already laid out for me. I think on these things daily, Amen.

Scripture:
So a man thinketh so is he. Proverbs 23:7.

Your Hearts Reflection

www.ingramcontent.com/pod-product-compliance
Lightning Source LLC
Chambersburg PA
CBHW050856150626
46549CB00013B/2424